I0796047

WELCOMING INTERIORS, BEAUTIFUL DESIGN

THE INVITING SOUTHERN HOME

WELCOMING INTERIORS, BEAUTIFUL DESIGN

LYNN LEE TERRY

Hoffman Media
2323 2nd Avenue North
Birmingham, AL 35203
hoffmanmedia.com

ISBN 979-8-9923852-4-3
Printed in China

83 press

Contents

Introduction

The South has long been a region defined by its rich cultural heritage, storied traditions, and deep-rooted sense of place. It is a place where architecture and interior design are not just aesthetic choices, but expressions of history, personality, and lifestyle. In *The Inviting Southern Home*, we take you on a visual journey through 19 extraordinary homes designed by some of the South's most respected interior designers and architects—each one a testament to the unique character and creativity of the region and designed to welcome family and friends.

From the classical elegance of a Virginia estate to the modern warmth of a Texas abode, these homes reflect a range of styles, yet all are grounded in a sense of Southern identity. They speak to a way of life that values comfort without compromise, beauty without pretense, and timelessness without rigidity. Of course, hospitality and entertaining are always top of mind for Southern decorators, with layered interiors and a lively host always ready to welcome you in.

This book brings together a rich tapestry of Southern homes that span a diverse range of styles—each distinct, yet all thoughtfully designed. From the timeless elegance of classic interiors to the clean lines and bold simplicity of modern spaces, these homes reflect the evolving spirit of Southern design. Curated residences showcase layered textures and collected pieces that tell deeply personal stories, while colorful homes embrace fearless palettes and vibrant patterns that breathe life into every room. Nestled among them are serene retreats—spaces designed to restore and recharge, often surrounded by nature and imbued with a sense of calm. Together, these homes reveal how style in the South is not defined by one look, but by a deep appreciation for comfort, character, and creativity.

Each chapter offers a behind-the-scenes look at the thoughtful design decisions that shape these remarkable interiors—spaces that blend old and new, tradition and innovation, local craftsmanship and global inspiration. Whether it's a historic renovation that breathes new life into ancestral walls or a contemporary build that reinterprets Southern vernacular, these homes share a commitment to quality, authenticity, and a deep respect for place.

Through stunning photography and insightful commentary, *The Inviting Southern Home* celebrates not only the designers and architects behind these homes, but also the stories of the families who live in them. It is our hope that these pages will inspire you—whether you're a designer, homeowner, or simply a lover of beautiful spaces—to see the South not as a monolithic style, but as a living, evolving design landscape.

Welcome to the heart of Southern design.

CLASSIC

Classic Collaboration

Ambitious ideas, such as a striking rotunda like the one designed by Thomas Jefferson at the University of Virginia, defined the overarching vision for this 13,000-square-foot project in Atlanta. To translate such lofty concepts into comfortable living spaces, the homeowners already had architect Keith Summerour of Summerour and Associates on board. Now they had their minds set on one designer, Barbara Westbrook of Westbrook Interiors. "The owners loved the look of the renovation at Old Edwards Inn, and Keith was responsible for that," says Westbrook. "We handled the interior detailing for the luxury suites at the inn, and that look epitomized what these clients wanted for their new home."

When Westbrook met with the homeowners, it came as no surprise to find the couple had a penchant for history and hospitality. "The husband went to UVA, so they loved the idea of honoring those ties with the rotunda in their home," says Westbrook. More Virginian influence came from Monticello and its Roman neoclassical designs, but the homeowners also wanted to temper the stateliness with warmth. "They wanted a welcoming place for their family," says the designer.

In a unified sort of divide-and-conquer manner, Westbrook crafted interior plans and palettes with a nod toward Colonial times, while Summerour worked to execute the home's architectural marvels. "I wanted to bring light and activity to the center of the house," says Summerour of the rotunda. He gave it "a sculptural element" that propelled the plans for the entire home, employing masterful tricks of the trade to make the most of the space. "As an example, the doors in the rotunda are curved, and the second floor is smaller with walls that slope inward, creating a sense of greater height," explains the architect.

Westbrook matched style to scale by combining inspiration from the Old Dominion and the Deep South. Antique pewter, crewelwork, rich wood tones, wrought iron, and turned legs appear throughout the home. Westbrook notes, "For us, it was about mixing styles—giving the house a stateliness that didn't feel too stiff or unapproachable."

Amid soaring arches and impressive molding, textures help define the refined vibe. Silk and chenille live alongside slipcovered sofas and burlap pillows. "I like things that have a feel when you touch them," says Westbrook.

She also put signature touches on the kitchen cabinetry and in the bathrooms. "I always include a few things that are unexpected and one-of-a-kind. Maybe it's something that was handmade or perhaps has a flange or a welted edge to give it that personal look."

Indeed, custom features define this timeless dwelling. From the octagonal dining room to the paneled-wood study to the oval pool, each element was shaped with intentionality and artistry. And with their vision now a reality, the owners can focus on family life in a home that offers historical character combined with the comforts for today's lifestyle.

In the study, artwork by John Folsom, titled Botany Bay Plantation Marsh Road, *inspires an earthy color palette. In the cypress-wrapped office, handcrafted pieces, such as a walnut writing desk, pair with rustic and refined details for a sense of subdued stateliness.*

The architect built hidden storage closets into the perimeter archways that lead to adjacent spaces such as the breakfast room. Here, Westbrook selected an oval chandelier in forged steel to illuminate a Gregorius Pineo table in a dry-aged walnut. "The rotunda's walls slope inward, which makes it seem higher than it actually is," notes Summerour. "And as another sleight of hand, I put in a window that is matched on the opposite side so it doubles the light coming into the center of the house."

"This kitchen is one of my favorites," says Westbrook. "It was a challenge to design because there were so many functions. The homeowners have busy lives, and they do the typical meals plus snack duty for the children and their friends. But they also wanted a full chef's kitchen with a deep fryer and steamer." The thick walnut butcher block was chosen for its beauty and durability. Leaded glass featured in select cabinet fronts brings a vintage touch to the room. Neutral walls yield an open, airy feel, and custom iron pendants with pleated shades continue to lighten the space.

The wood beams continue onto the covered porch, creating a seamless transition from indoors to out. The grandeur of the family room's soaring ceiling finds balance through carefully edited furnishings and accessories, including artwork by James McLaughlin Way.

MALTERIE
LOUIS
VILAIN

White terry cloth adds a hint of pretty practicality to the ottoman in the primary bath. To ensure plenty of light in the master bath, the designer included a bell lantern in bronze, along with double-light sconces in antique nickel with paper shades. The primary suite relies on muted tones, rich wooden pieces, and iron accents for a refined yet restful setting. Matelassé upholstery on the chairs and ottoman pairs well with the mohair rug to soften the surroundings.

1871
24

Island Style

Designer Will Huff of Huff-Dewberry was hired to decorate a client's Atlanta home, but before they started the project was put on hold. A few years passed, and she called again. "She was a widow, and in that time she had met an amazing man, gotten married, and was building a house on Amelia Island with him," says Huff. Together with the architecture firm Spitzmiller & Norris, Huff helped create a casually elegant retreat, perfect for hosting family, grandchildren, and even granddogs.

The husband runs his business from home, frequently holding meetings, while the couple also hosts fundraisers. "A very narrow lot presented a challenge," says Huff. "The architects were masterful in maximizing space for large gatherings and capturing spectacular views of protected marshes and the Intracoastal Waterway."

The living room, with its 18-foot ceiling and multiple seating areas, could have felt impersonal, but Huff incorporated warm textures and refined silhouettes to create a welcoming atmosphere. "In our initial design meeting, the client stated that she wanted the house to reflect a casual, happy, and sophisticated feeling with fine things sprinkled throughout," says Huff. "And she wanted it all in shades of blue."

Blue envelops the dining room, with textured wallpaper setting off a play of wood furniture and gold accents. Huff layered two different-scale checks on the table for visual interest, and mahogany antiques ground the space. White painted Chippendale chairs surround the table, while a gold chandelier adds sparkle. Huff also designed hand-painted panels depicting local marshland scenes.

In the kitchen, double islands allow guests to hang out with the cook without impeding dinner prep. A large breakfast table seats eight comfortably, with a banquette allowing children and grandchildren to pile in for family meals. Spill-proof leather covers the seat, with an overscale check on the back and chairs to connect the space to the other rooms.

A long hallway to the main bedroom gave the architects an opportunity to dazzle. "We imagined that walking from the bedroom through a trellised gallery, with its large windows, would heighten the connection to the natural surroundings," says Rick Spitzmiller.

The clients wanted the bedroom to have the feeling of being in a cloud. To that end, Huff chose ethereal hues of blue and cream. Exquisite details in the fabric treatments add dimension to the restrained design. "We used an embroidered fabric on the outside of the bed's cornice and cut it into strips to edge the draperies," says Huff. "I think we accomplished what she was going for."

FLORENCE

In the lofty living room, the client's antique garniture set takes pride of place on the mantel, which was custom-sized to accommodate it. A variety of fabrics, from velvet to a tiger print, differentiate the three seating areas.

In the study, the architects created a pattern of hewn beams to distinguish the workspace from the rest of the house. A corner banquette in the living room sits below a wall of favorite Audubon prints.

In the dining room, Huff layered checks in varying sizes from a Schumacher collection. He chose a textured wallpaper by Waterhouse to avoid competing with the hand-painted panels he commissioned with local flora and fauna.

In the kitchen and breakfast room, a pair of islands and banquette offer space for large gatherings.

The guest house features a generous seating area and, in a departure from the main house, a leaf green palette. The guesthouse bedroom features a Sanderson botanical fabric.

Spitzmiller & Norris designed the custom latticework pattern to give the hallway to the primary bedroom the feeling of a garden room. "The clients wanted their bedroom to feel like being in a cloud," says Huff. A Cowtan & Tout velvet covers the two-sided chaise. An embroidered fabric by Brunschwig & Fils edges the drapery fabric.

Soft blues offer a tranquil retreat that seamlessly blends with the exterior views.

To the Manor Born

Experiences abroad can deeply influence one's vision when designing a dream home. For Stan Dixon and Jackye Lanham's client, time spent in the Cotswolds during her youth left a lasting impression. Dixon, who studied architecture in England, and Lanham, an Anglophile, embraced this aesthetic during the design process.

The home's facade reflects British manor house influences, featuring symmetrical gables, a pair of chimneys, and a warm mix of limestone and unique brick with a mortar wash finish. The elegant casement windows with timber frames and a Vermont slate roof further enhance its charm. Inside, the design draws on the work of renowned British architect Edwin Lutyens, particularly his design for Castle Drogo, with coffered ceilings, limestone mantels, and a custom European oak kitchen surface. "Lutyens had large tables in his kitchens, and we incorporated that concept with a comfortable 36-inch prep surface," says Dixon. "It adds warmth and creates a more collected feel, especially with the timber casement windows."

Lanham incorporated the client's fine collection of antique furniture and artwork, softening the heavier Tudor-style pieces. The de Gournay wallcovering departs from the dark tones typical of many English country houses. The custom finish features muted blues and greens on a warm tea-colored background.

To avoid a heavy, dated feel, Lanham introduced unexpected elements throughout the house for this young family. For example, a lively teal-painted bench in a connecting space was inspired by breezeways in Italian houses, offering a playful contrast to a traditional table. The color of the bench echoed the client's chinoiserie screen and was paired with matching painted wooden floor lamps. "The bench makes a dramatic statement when viewed from the backyard," says Lanham.

In addition to the custom bench, Lanham selected distinctive light fixtures, including globe pendants inspired by Moroccan lanterns and a faded ocher two-tiered chandelier for the study. These touches balance the English-inspired elements with modern flair.

The back of the house is equally captivating, with a long loggia framed by Voussoir arches, which Dixon notes are typical of English ecclesiastical and academic buildings. The detailing where the arches meet the columns was one of the most challenging design elements. For the loggia's floor, the team sourced reclaimed Cotswold stone from English gardens. The space connects to a pristine lawn, surrounded by a crushed stone courtyard and pathways designed by Atlanta landscape architect John Howard.

Every detail of the home, from the arches to the furnishings, reflects the timeless English sensibility that has inspired designers for centuries. Much like Lutyen's Castle Drogo, this Atlanta home is a design masterpiece destined to stand the test of time.

The living room reveals a sophisticated creamy palette punctuated by shades of blue, including a collection of blue-and-white porcelain.

INSPIRED BY TRADITION
ONE MAN'S FOLLY

A specially colored de Gournay wallcovering graces the dining room, while elegant millwork draws the eye up to appreciate the design.

A round table separates two seating areas in the family room, highlighted by a chandelier with lively teal custom shades.

Decorating Master Class

The French oak island was inspired by tables that Dixon saw at Castle Drogo in England. Arches in Kansas limestone speak to the English-inspired architecture and define the outdoor entertaining space.

Elegant floor-to-ceiling doors allow abundant light into the primary bedroom. In a connecting space that leads to the primary bedroom, Lanham placed a curvaceous bench accompanied by a chinoiserie screen.

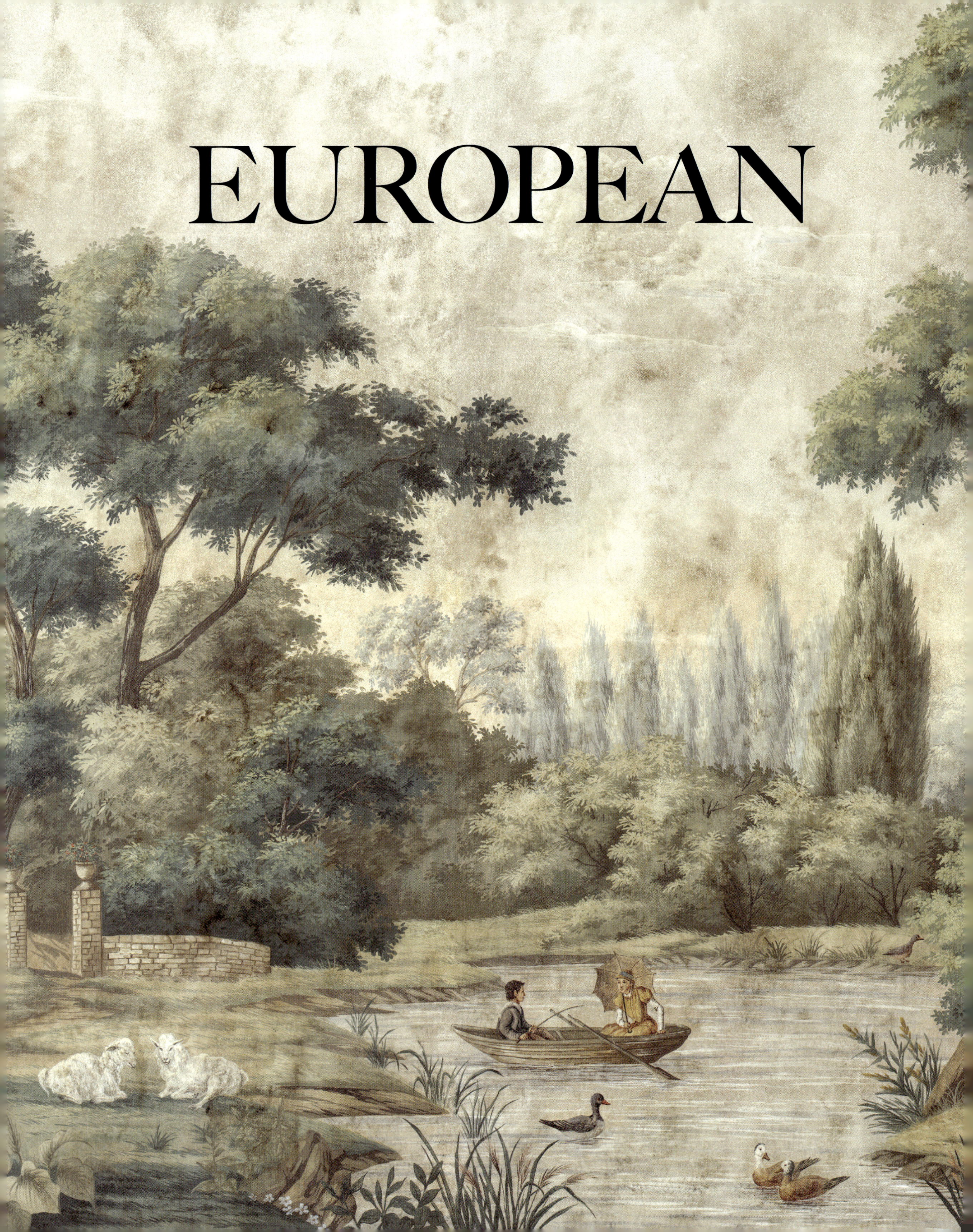
EUROPEAN

Passport to Italy

When a dear friend with homes in New York and Paris approached John Oetgen to create a new house for her in Atlanta, he imagined a space that would evoke far-flung locations and historic dwellings. "She is an artist, a philanthropist, and a woman of great style," Oetgen says of his friend of over 40 years. "I wanted to give her the sense of an Italian apartment in a dusty old palazzo." Since the space was an unfinished shell when the client bought it, Oetgen had free rein to establish the lofty proportions and simple furniture arrangements suggestive of a Venetian palace.

The rooms all radiate off an oval center hall, where statues of sheep rest on marble floors. Oetgen took the client's beloved 18th-century prints of an Indian Raj hunting scene, blew them up to 8 feet tall, and had them printed on vinyl wallpaper. He then built the paneling to frame them. An old rusted wrought-iron table with a stone top from France serves as a drop-off spot for bags and keys while lending a hint of the outdoors to the transitional space.

In the living room, everything is designed to transport the client and her guests to romantic locales. Minimal moldings and tall windows, plainly dressed in roman shades, add to the Italianate vibe. "The room needed to seem as if it overlooked the Vatican or St. Mark's Square," says Oetgen. "I wanted to create a sense of old minimalism. There is no regard to what is flea market and what is fine."

That dusty effect is in full expression in the dining room. "My goal was to design a space that feels like an old Dutch painting," says Oetgen. "The chairs don't match, and none of the fabrics are new. The ceiling treatment is especially distinctive. It's very similar to that of rural Italian houses, where they stack beams horizontally and then vertically and then add the roof." A smaller dining room is used for more intimate gatherings, with antique Scandinavian chairs and a table occupying an otherwise bare space.

The cavernous master bedroom, with 12-foot ceilings and streaming natural light, is grounded by the furniture arrangement. Oetgen designed a tall headboard and hung an antique tapestry behind it, creating a room-within-a-room effect. The substantial bedside chest and a carved-wood bench at the foot of the bed enhance the look. A frothy chandelier the client bought in the Netherlands crowns the arrangement. "She likes a good old sparkly chandelier," says Oetgen. The designer's words radiate the warmth of genuine friendship, surely the most ideal of working relationships. And the results clearly speak for themselves.

Caravaggio

The oval entry hall is the nexus of the house, with all the rooms radiating off of it. Stone sheep garden statues rest under an outdoor table. Oetgen enlarged his client's cherished Raj prints and framed them with woodwork. An antique French demilune sits beneath a collection of antique prints.

Oetgen designed the dining room's ceiling to evoke an Italian farmhouse. "The chairs do not match, and none of the fabrics are new," says Oetgen. The client's china collection from her world travels fills a cabinet.

In the living room, spare arrangements and casual placement of furniture pieces have the effect of a centuries-old residence. Oetgen calls it "a touch of old minimalism." The artwork is a mix of souvenirs and investment pieces.

The small breakfast room is furnished with Scandinavian antiques. The kitchen is simple with herringbone wood floors and antique ornaments on the countertops. Antique Wedgwood holds silverware for daily use.

The study houses hunt pictures and memorabilia from the client's previous house in England "We used dark velvets and textures in the room with lots of wood grain and clubby English antiques," says Oetgen. He designed the guest room around a painted Italian screen and its radiant plum color.

Oetgen arranged the furniture in the primary bedroom to enhance the 12-foot ceiling height. An antique tapestry behind the tall headboard lends a monumental scale to the room. Collections ranging from Staffordshire dogs to Asian artifacts reinforce the sense of a retreat for a world traveler. Mirrored doors throughout the primary suite add old-world glamour.

ROME
SALADINO VILLA
VENEZIA

French Influence

If you ask a design expert for advice on the most worthy investment related to furnishing your house, the answer is often something like this: "Buy the best you can afford." The response from Dallas designer Cathy Kincaid is similar, but her reason has nothing to do with investment value or resale projections. For her, it's all about quality and timelessness. Her affinity for reusing and repurposing is evident throughout her portfolio, as well as in her home in the Preston Hollow area.

The property belonged to an old friend, so Kincaid already had a firm foundation on which to build the design plan. At first the client was looking for "a little nip and tuck" to update the home, but as the work progressed and hidden potential was uncovered, the project became more extensive. "There were Country French overtones but lots of quality furniture," says Kincaid. "We diluted that look and freshened it up so that the feeling is more timeless." Antique Swedish and modern pieces bring a fresh feel to the dining and living rooms. Fabric details that reveal Kincaid's precise and creative eye make every bit of upholstery unique and new. And patterned fabric and paper on walls and furniture come together to create a chorus of color and life, transcending potentially discordant tones and prints. She credits this proficiency in juxtaposition to her mentor, Fort Worth designer Joe Minton, who encouraged her to use imperfectly matching colors to create a tension that stimulates the eye and shakes things up a bit.

To accomplish this, Kincaid reused the best of what was available—and reupholstering or painting if necessary—to bring new life to dated pieces. She also encouraged the homeowner to invest in pieces that serve current needs. "We call it a fruit basket turnover," she says—it's about preserving the best of the past while investing in the future.

Kincaid also called upon friend and colleague Charlie Birdsong, who has a solid reputation for styling and assembling collections. He created intricately detailed lampshades to coordinate with Kincaid's choices of window treatments and trims. He also combined collections of antique plates and paintings, brackets, and barometers atop patterned paper for a beguiling display the homeowner adored. Kincaid was thus able to revive the home and introduce pieces and finishes that infused it with luxury and personality. Though humble in its beginnings, this project evolved into something grand, giving the homeowner a dream dwelling place to enjoy for years to come.

There's a Swedish lightness to the painted chairs and bleached demilune tables that works particularly well in Dallas, as do subtly striped wallpaper, carpet, and window treatments.

Kincaid flanked the fireplace with mirrors from John Rosselli to "evoke windows and expand the space," she says. The owner already had the rug, so Kincaid repeated its blue tones throughout the room with upholstery, window treatments, and a collection of Chinese export plates. For a fresh twist, Kincaid added a mid-century, glass-topped coffee table.

CHARLOTTE MOSS GARDEN INSPIRATIONS
MONET A RETROSPECTIVE

In the breakfast room, a hand-painted textile and antique Delft plates preside over a painted bench with upholstered cushions. Says Kincaid, "They just soften the space and transform the piece." The drop-leaf oak table accommodates the family for intimate dinners and extends to seat more for special occasions with guests. An antique brass Dutch chandelier visually warms the family room, but it's the upholstered furniture that makes it ideal for kicking back. A collection of Texas landscape paintings evokes the outdoors.

Kincaid selected the colors for the custom Bennison print according to the homeowner's collections.

All in the Mix

Sit down with Ann Wolf, and the Texas-based designer will tell you she was greatly influenced by her East Coast upbringing. Raised in Manhattan, she and her husband have lived in the Lone Star State for three decades, but her roots remain evident in her designs. "I think I bring an East Coast sensibility to my work. I'm always really inspired by American furnishings, and I love to mix pattern and color."

This style caught the attention of a young Houston family who hired Wolf for their new build in the Memorial neighborhood. "The wife wanted a traditional house, and she liked my aesthetic," Wolf says. Early in the home's design phase, she joined forces with the late architect Reagan Miller. "Having input on the plans leads to a better outcome," Wolf notes, emphasizing her focus on practical details like window and outlet placements to optimize function.

Being involved from the start gave Wolf insight into the family's lifestyle and priorities, allowing her to design spaces that supported their needs. For example, she recommended dual islands in the kitchen, enabling the parents to cook and prep at one while the kids worked on homework or art projects at the other. "The kitchen is the heartbeat of the house, especially for a young family, and this setup lets them be together," says Wolf.

Beyond function, the home offers visual intrigue, with each space revealing layers of design that encourage discovery. "I love room-by-room discovery to create continuity," Wolf explains, highlighting how elements like a collection of antique Delft pottery in the kitchen tie into the blue, yellow, and green palette in the family room. "We built collections of art and pottery to make it feel layered from the start," she adds. Her love for fabrics is evident too, with a rug in the family room that complements the kitchen's backsplash.

Upstairs, the children's rooms reflect their personalities, with vibrant yellow, blue, and hot pink patterns chosen by the kids themselves. "I had a lot of fun in the kids' rooms," Wolf says, ensuring the home's overall design flow continues throughout.

Wolf's approach also includes mixing styles for added visual appeal. "I like to mix mid-century modern pieces into traditional designs to keep things fresh and interesting," she says. This is seen in the entry, where a 1950s table contrasts with classic heavy molding and paneling. Similarly, a Victorian wicker chair and ottoman with antique textiles blend seamlessly with a contemporary Alexander Calder piece above the mantel.

Wolf worked with an art consultant to select personal pieces for the home, including paintings, sculptures, and photographs. "It's all about making the design feel true to the client," she says. The result is a home that balances functionality, personal style, and design continuity.

RAUSCHENBERG
MARY LYNN KOTZ

In the living room, a decorative paint treatment in a dusty apricot shade covers the walls. Over the sofa hangs a contemporary photograph of an antique painting restoration shop in Italy, thus mixing the new with the old. The work at the right, by artist Ethan Cook, features textiles woven together to appear like a canvas, and the coffee table is a piece crafted by famed father-son metal artisans and furniture makers, Philip and Kelvin LaVerne.

"I LIKE TO MIX MID-CENTURY MODERN PIECES INTO TRADITIONAL DESIGNS TO KEEP THINGS INTERESTING AND FRESH." —ANN WOLF

A scenic de Gournay wallpaper elevates the formality of the dining room. The adjacent hallway leads to a moody-hued deep blue bar with an Alex Katz print visible from the doorway.

Wolf's masterful mix of pattern, color, and time periods is perhaps most evident in the family room. "I love fabrics, and I like to work with a client to build collections of art and pottery to make a home feel layered from the start," the designer says.

AGNES MARTIN
HENRI MATISSE
MATISSE/DIEBENKORN
SPLENDOR
Matisse Cut-outs

A wallcovering and chandelier bring what Wolf calls "a maximalist explosion of color" to the breakfast nook. A porcelain collection lends color and character in the timeless white kitchen.

NEAR & FAR

The primary suite is marked by a shift to a more subdued palette. Wolf notes she was guided by the floral hand block-printed Lee Jofa fabric to create her "vision of a soft, restful space." Here, a grasscloth covers the walls while a framed quilt acts as art over the bed. The feel carries through to the classic bath.

MODERN

Color Craving

From the outside, the stately presence of a historic Georgian-style manse perched high above Richmond, Virginia's James River appears remarkably untouched by the hands of time. But step inside, and your senses are surprisingly overtaken by a fresh modern vibe pulsating with color. The homeowners, a young couple with four children, recognized the house's potential but needed more space and a contemporary refresh. They hired designer Janie Molster for a four-year renovation project, which would add a main bedroom, family room, outdoor terraces, and a lower-level living area.

Molster embraced the home's traditional architecture, infusing it with youthful, playful designs. She incorporated bold color palettes—rich purples, candy pink, magenta, and marigold—giving each room its own visual energy. Despite this modernization, Molster respected the home's original bones, avoiding large open spaces and keeping kitchen, living, and dining areas separate.

"We worked on every detail, from materials to finishes," Molster says. "It was about understanding their lifestyle and exposing them to new design ideas that reflected who they are." The couple stayed highly involved throughout the process, making the design journey collaborative. Molster and designer Robyn Framme enjoyed frequent meetings with them to refine preferences and expedite decisions.

The home blends old and new, with antique pieces chosen carefully to complement the modern aesthetic. Notable finds include an antique settee in the entrance hall that contrasts with graphic wallpaper and leather-fringed sconces, and a Swedish dining table paired with hot-pink draperies and a gilded chandelier. In the family room, a custom fringed chandelier adds texture to the earthy palette.

The spaces are designed to be flexible for a busy family. With frequent parties and children's birthdays in mind, each room is multifunctional. "This house reflects my clients' taste, not mine," Molster notes. "Our goal was to create something unique, and I hope its style is undefinable."

Every inch of the home radiates luxury, from opulent fabrics like velvet and silk to bespoke touches that enhance the sense of comfort and style. Through thoughtful design, the home has become a vibrant, family-centered space, rich in both character and color.

Designer Janie Molster empowers the living room with a modern infusion of seductive purple and marigold hues. The living room's glamorous statement pieces include a glossy organic coffee table that mirrors the curvaceous shape of a plush lavender velvet sofa. Preceding pages: An antique settee in the foyer is one of Molster's favorite finds.

A master of mixing the modern with the antique, Molster energizes the dining room by pairing vibrant pink ombré draperies and a luminous gold-embellished chandelier with the sublime simplicity of an antique Swedish dining table. Saturated in a captivating shade of deep teal, the library makes an exotic reading retreat with its cozy fireplace.

BEATON

The solarium offers a sunny spot to curl up for a nap. A causal dining table serves indoor and outdoor guests with effortless ease.

Outfitted with quiet neutral shades, dark fabrics, and masculine leathers, the family room provides an earthy palette cleanser for the home's otherwise colorful aesthetic.

WORLD of MURIEL BRANDOLINI

Awash in shades of cotton candy, rosy pink, lavender, and turquoise, the daughters' bedrooms and a playroom emit a fresh, modern feel. "I loved working with the youngest daughter on her adorable pink room," says Molster. "Still in preschool when we began the project, she absorbed so much by spending time with us and has now developed her own little aesthetic."

Layered in pale pinks, soft lavenders, and luxe golds, the light-filled primary suite exudes an air of chic sophistication with a modern touch.

"OUR GOAL WAS TO CREATE SOMETHING UNIQUE, AND I HOPE ITS STYLE IS UNDEFINABLE."
—JANIE MOLSTER

A mudroom splashed with vibrant color and modern accents paves the way to the lush landscape outside. "The family's favorite spots migrate with the seasons," says Molster. "The terrace fireplace is a draw in the cooler months."

All About the Views

Washington, D.C., designer Mary Douglas Drysdale epitomizes the interior designer ideal, with longtime clients returning to her for every transition in their lives. For a recent project, the 11th for a sophisticated and well-traveled couple, Drysdale crafted a glamorous condominium in a Bethesda, Maryland, high-rise. "My first project for them, a shingle-style house in Maine, was more than 20 years ago," says Drysdale. "That was followed by a Colonial-style house in Potomac and other historic grand houses in Maryland. I have seen their family expand and then their children leave home and begin their own lives. This wonderful condominium represents the empty nester phase of their story."

The pair tasked Drysdale with a redesign of the layout to take advantage of the 10th-floor views of downtown Bethesda. "My aim was to create a more modern plan in this very new luxury property and to strongly engage the inside with the outside," she says. "The terrace serves as a second living room for eight months of the year." The living room's seating arrangement is streamlined and low, leading the eye to the terrace and the treetops beyond. Drysdale kept the scheme monochromatic, with fabrics and carpet in complementary shades of blue. "It's the wife's favorite color," says Drysdale. "It worked well in the strongly sunlit space. The blue holds the center of activity together, while the cabinetry and walls are white. It's a rich center with a perimeter that fades into the clouds."

A notable artwork by D.C. artist Linn Myers features prominently in the foyer, a classic Drysdale touch. "Since the piece is not intended to be framed, I created a niche to show this unframed work on canvas," she says. At each end of the niche, shelves display artwork, including a collection of photographs by another local artist, Wendy Concannon. "We wanted to make that focal point lively and active when viewed from the kitchen."

Because an enclosed dining room would have interrupted the view, Drysdale encouraged the couple to opt for an open plan, with a dining table that serves as a de facto entry hall table and garden stools for flexible seating. White leather chairs stacked in a nearby closet can easily be swapped for the stools when needed and the stools moved outside. "We wanted pieces that could work easily indoors and out," says Drysdale. The couple routinely dine at the kitchen's second island, with its great views and proximity to the work area. A custom paint color, like a thunder cloud, shrouds the kitchen and creates a warm environment, especially at night with the room richly lit.

The bedroom also takes a turn in palette, with pale wood tones in the paneling, bedding, and rug. It's a streamlined room but soft as well, with comforting textures and clean lines. Like the other rooms, it is the perfect setting for a couple shifting the focus of their domestic life back upon each other.

BAZAAR 150 YEARS

In the entry, a Jansen chest sits beneath a series of works by Donald Sultan. A large unframed blue canvas by Linn Meyers is set into a custom-built niche to greet visitors in the entry. A series of smaller works by Wendy Concannon perches on shelves at the end of the structural column Drysdale used to divide the space.

In the living room, a large sectional keeps a low profile to draw the eye to the view beyond. Garden stools by Janus et Cie at the dining table can be swapped for leather dining chairs stashed in a nearby closet for guests requiring more comfort.

A kitchen island serves as command central for the couple, for sipping coffee, checking emails, and enjoying the view. A rich custom paint color lets the kitchen cabinetry recede against the treetops outside the kitchen. Multiple seating areas on the terrace allow it to serve as a second living room most of the year.

In the bedroom, paneled walls and built-in nightstands reduce visual clutter and provide serene surroundings.

Big Easy Breezy

When Houstonian Michael Whalen bought a storied house in the French Quarter, he asked Houston designer Katie Scott to manage the renovation and decoration. Being a New Orleans native, Scott leapt at the opportunity to refresh the historic interiors and create a modern, luxurious Big Easy retreat. She was not familiar with the Lalaurie House, so she looked for more information at a local bookstore, where she was directed to the section on haunted houses. "I wondered what I had gotten myself into," she recalls. But the lavish mansion proved too alluring to pass up.

Built in the early 1800s, the Lalaurie House had survived scandal, neglect, and hauntings before actor Nicholas Cage bought it in 2007. When Scott set about giving the house a fresh new look, she took inspiration from the fun-loving yet grandly historic neighborhood. "We wanted to create a sexy, burlesque, French Quarter feel—rich in color with modern flourishes," she says. New plaster, lacquered walls, and restored crown moldings contribute to a jazzy, upbeat scheme.

One challenge in decorating a house of this period is adapting the formal spaces to the expectations of comforts for a modern lifestyle. Parlors, ballrooms, and foyers were common in these homes, but they did not encourage lingering. Scott solved that dilemma with intimate arrangements of upholstered furniture, one of the most effective ways to bring warmth to an imposing room. "Layering and diversifying textures is key to bringing comfort to grand spaces," she says. "Custom curtains and rugs play vital roles in adding volume and depth."

A spirit of fun reigns over the house, with a daring palette—black lacquered walls in the study, a pink-and-red confection in the living room, a kitchen with blush lacquered walls—and modern art in place of the expected period artwork. At every turn there are moments of surprise and whimsy, such as the pink tufted "social" in the kitchen and the lit-from-within coffee tables in the parlor. A colorful piece of modern artwork is framed in the reflection of an antique gilt mirror, leaving no doubt that this house was made for ignoring the rules. "As I imagined how this home would be used, I pictured guests hanging out in the kitchen, drinking Bloody Marys with the windows to the balcony open and a parade rolling by," she says. "The kitchen's tufted 'social' came to mind as the perfect spot to gather."

In the formal parlor, lacquered black to set off the intricate plasterwork, contrasts are striking. "I chose the selenite coffee table for its resemblance to an iceberg—aglow and lending a cooling effect to the walls," says Scott. Abiding with the balance of textures, leather and fur sofas provide natural warmth against the marble floors and coffee table. "I love the tension that is created between two opposing forces," says the designer. "I see best when old and new collide. It's electric!" Having banished the gloom from the historic home, Scott added one last touch for good measure. "As a gift for my client, I brought in a priest to bless the house."

William Claxton NEW ORLEANS 1960
TASCHEN

Black lacquered walls set off the ornate crown moldings and carved doors. Modern artwork by Bernd Haussmann, Ken Tate, and Susan Dory balances out the historic architecture. Draped chandeliers from Hudson add a ghostly note.

STAN SHAFFER

Scott takes a modern approach to the traditional living room with classic New Orleans furniture pumped up in proportion and palette. A red tufted sofa and commodious chairs by Christopher Guy offer a welcome and comfortable change to the more expected settee-and-bergères configuration. A vintage Yves Saint Laurent jewelry case sits beneath an antique trumeau mirror, both from Jon Vaccari.

A small recess off the living room serves as a lounge area. In the hallway, artwork by Roi James is framed by the intricate doorway.

Clearly not designed for heavy-duty cooking, the kitchen features blush lacquered walls and black silk taffeta curtains that puddle on the floor. A pink velvet-covered "social" adds a dash of whimsy to the luxurious kitchen. With its gray plastered walls and restored plaster friezes, the dining room emits a more serious tone than the rest of the home. Chairs are upholstered with python skin.

A guest room features a baroque treatment with rich damask-covered walls and a black lacquered ceiling. Scott custom-designed the bed. The Venetian chair pays tribute to another festive city.

COLORFUL

Classic Meets Colorful

"Heritage and tradition are very important to me. They are fantastic family values my mother instilled in me," says designer Edith-Anne Duncan. These values are evident in the Blacksburg, Virginia, home she shares with her husband, David, and their college-aged twins, Paul and Georgia-Kathryn. Inside, an air of gentility mixes with a jovial flair of modernity. "I wanted this house to be warm and inviting yet colorful and happy. I created a very positive and upbeat feel that is also connected to my roots," Duncan says of the blend that perfectly encompasses her style.

After living in a previous home for 18 years, the couple decided to build again, choosing the property next door. Duncan had spent years collecting design inspiration, and this new home became a "design laboratory" for experimenting with fresh ideas. Growing up in North Carolina, Duncan's love for design was nurtured by her grandparents and father, sparking a lifelong passion for color. "My grandmother would take me to the Lilly Pulitzer store every year for a new dress," she recalls. This early exposure to bold color choices is reflected throughout the home, with hues from nearly every color palette, anchored by warm tones of pink, shrimp, and red, creating cohesion from room to room. Duncan has a particular affinity for the finishing details, like art, rugs, fabrics and trimmings, which elevate the entire design.

While the interior embraces boldness, Duncan wanted the exterior to exude timeless charm. "I wanted it to look like it had evolved over time," she says. The design features a central "main house" flanked by two wings, one housing the primary suite and the other Duncan's studio office, which doubles as a dining room. The studio, inspired by Aerin Lauder's pool house, is painted in neutral whites, providing a serene backdrop for fabric and design selections. The space also hosts gatherings, where festive décor adds personality and vibrancy to the neutral foundation.

Duncan is a firm believer in adding a surprise element to each space. For example, in her husband's study, the unexpected marbled wallpaper on the ceiling creates visual interest on the room's fifth wall. However, she also takes a sensible approach to storage and organization. "I like things to be accessible so I can enjoy them," she says, referring to her sterling silver collection. Displayed in a modern cabinet with glass-front doors, the collection is both functional and beautiful, embodying her philosophy that design should be practical and aesthetically pleasing.

This home is a perfect balance of modern livability and timeless beauty, where every detail serves both form and function—an inviting space that's as vibrant and colorful as its designer.

LOUIS VUITTON

A blue-and-white scenic wallpaper by Fromental greets guests in the front entry, while pink upholstered cubes from CR Laine add cheer. The blue hue in the study was inspired by Ford Motors. "My husband David's family has owned a Ford dealership in town for more than 60 years," Duncan says.

PHOEBE HOWARD The Joy of Decorating
RICHMOND
PALM BEACH

The family room's blue palette is an extension of the adjoining breakfast room. Since the gathering space receives daily use, Duncan prioritized comfortable seating and added stools that move throughout the room easily to accommodate a crowd. In the background, her collection of silver serving pieces can be seen in glass-front cabinets in the kitchen.

Duncan chose an all-white palette for the kitchen surfaces, knowing she would add in pops of color with the drapery fabric and seasonal décor. Drawers, rather than upper cabinets, house all the kitchen's essentials, a detail the designer notes is ideal for ease of use. The barrel-vaulted ceiling lends an airy feel, while a mix of silver and gold finishes provide polish. The breakfast room features an approachable combination of bistro chairs and a tulip table paired with a geometric drum-shade light fixture. The work over the mantel is by South Carolina artist Kelly Pelfrey, while the bowl of cherries near the table is by Amy Crews.

Duncan's dining room pulls double duty as her office during the day, with the dining table transforming into a conference table for client presentations. A treillage wall treatment, which was inspired by Aerin Lauder's pool house, coupled with views of the outdoor area and golf course beyond add to the open-air feel.

INSPIRED BY COLOR

The Duncans' daughter's room is outfitted with Laura Park bedding and a bedskirt and window treatment in Brunschwig & Fils's "Les Touches" fabric. The spacious guest room is a vibrant escape with a fretwork wallpaper that serves as a statement-making backdrop. "I recommend spending the night in your guest room from time to time to see what would make it more comfortable and if there's anything that a guest might need while there," the designer says. The elevator features wallpaper from Lee Jofa's Hunt Slonem Collection. "You are only there for such a short time; it should be a fun space," the designer notes.

In the primary bedroom, a mirrored wall echoes the room's mural wallpaper throughout the space. Vivid green and berry accents stand out against its silvery gray hue. Duncan played with scale by choosing an oversized geometric pattern for the custom rug alongside a smaller print for the drapes and chair.

Passion for Color

With five children, Julie and Mike Holmes needed a spacious home. Designer Kelley Proxmire, who had worked with them previously, introduced the couple to architect David Neumann when they bought an empty lot in Vienna, Virginia. Neumann's traditional style shaped a sizable house with six bedrooms, framed to allow bold use of color. Beautiful arched openings between rooms created flow without closing them off.

"The challenge of an open-plan design is to distinguish each space from the next," says Proxmire of the palette she used to separate spaces that flow into one another. "I do a floor plan and a color scheme," she says. "Then I figure out how to blend them and mix in neutrals and textures." Fabric swatches help her work out the scale of patterns, but the overriding consideration for this project was practicality. "With five kids and a dog, it had to be pretty but functional," she says. Indoor/outdoor fabrics were a must, as well as performance rugs used in high traffic areas. The visitor gets a healthy dose of caution-flung-to-the-wind upon entering the house, with its elegant Georgian door opening into a chinoiserie confection of a foyer with jonquil yellow wallpaper lining the walls and staircase. "It is bold," says Proxmire, "but it didn't take much convincing to get Julie to agree." The yellow carries through to the dining room as a counterpoint to the ebullient green chinoiserie wallpaper, lining the seats of upholstered dining chairs.

A master of mixing blue and green, Proxmire uses both to great effect in the family room with indigo chairs and fern green sofas, which energize the soothing white room. "I like to flip the primary colors so that no room is exactly the same as another," she says. In the paneled library, green takes center stage, with lacquered paneling and gray accents spiked with dashes of blue. In the kitchen, blue reigns with cabinets painted cobalt and a pair of islands offering space for both meals and homework.

In the children's bedrooms, personal preferences dictate the intensity of the palette, with some choosing soft pastels and others opting for bold hues. They're all pretty and all parent-approved, but each reflects the occupant's taste in a wonderfully specific manner. Throughout the house, Proxmire wove a story of the family through patterns, colors, and love, creating spaces that are both functional and deeply personal.

In the dining room, Brunschwig & Fils wallpaper sets a festive atmosphere for entertaining, with a chinoiserie mirror playing off the Oriental theme. In the entry, dark floors and woodwork give the staircase definition.

Built-in cabinets frame a niche for a second seating area in the living room with collected ceramics adorning the shelves.

In the library, Farrow & Ball's Calke Green on the walls creates an oasis of peace and calm. In the family room, which connects to the living room through pretty arched openings, Proxmire's favorite color combination of blue and green energizes the gathering space. White grasscloth wallcovering is laminated and treated for stain resistance. The custom lampshade on a green gourd lamp adds a sense of fun.

The large kitchen is the hub of family activity, with two islands painted a vivid blue providing space for meals, crafts, and homework. Lanterns with a scalloped detail add a flourish overhead. The breakfast room includes a banquette for flexible seating.

Each child had design input for their bedroom, with some choosing vivid hues and others soft pastels. In the parents' room, fresh green fabrics play off subdued blues for a restful retreat.

Carolina Calling

When a young couple and their children decided to make a nearly 100-year-old home their full-time residence, they knew it would require a special kind of redesign—one that would honor its unique history while also giving it a more functional layout and modern conveniences. Nestled in rural South Carolina—on land primed for producing peaches, pecans, and peppers—Stately Oaks is a family-run farm that exudes classic charm. From the Spanish moss swaying from the towering trees and the creeping fig running along the steps to the wide front porch and prominent columns, the house fits in perfectly among the landscape the deep South is so widely known for.

The home's architectural style can be described as a revival of Southern Federal and, like so many historic houses, had a few quirks and a tricky layout not suitable for today. The homeowners entrusted interior designer James Farmer to address these issues and completely update the interiors. "We started with the kitchen," says Farmer. "Older kitchens used to be smokehouses or would have been detached from the main house—they were not the comfortable hearts of the home we enjoy now." Once the modern kitchen was added on, the design team also rearranged the entire floor plan to a more traditional style. "When a homeowner asks for a big kitchen, I always remind them that the bigger the kitchen the bigger the mess," he adds. "Scale is very important, and by keeping a space proportional to the rest of the home, it forces everyone to spill out of the kitchen and into the other rooms."

The new floor plan includes a wide center hall with the parlor on the left and dining room on the right. The dining room now opens into the sunroom, foyer, and family room and gets natural light coming in from four sides. The flow of the home perfectly represents what Farmer refers to as an "unapologetic mix" that Southern décor is famous for. "I love that it's a formal dining room, but the furniture includes a painted table and upholstered seats, and it opens up to a room filled with wicker. That's what I love about the South," says the designer. "We mix the high with the low, and it gives it what I call the 'salt on the chocolate chip cookie'—that extra kick."

For the color palette, Farmer knew from the beginning he wanted to use a blend of greens and creams. The neutral yet bright combination allowed him to select shades that ranged from ivory to olive and created a gentle backdrop for the bolder furnishing selections, like the twin terra-cotta sofas in the family room. The two main colors are used throughout the entire house—whether it's the wall, ceiling, or trim color—and that, as Farmer says, represents the magic of interior design. "I loved that these clients really trusted us, because it allowed us to have a really wonderful collaboration," says the designer. "That trust, combined with our attention to scale and space, made everything work out beautifully. I always joke that interior design is a lot like football—it's just a game of inches and yards. If you take a foot here and a yard there...next thing you know, touchdown."

THE FRENCH DOG Rachael Hale
THE STYLISH LIFE TENNIS teNeues
Hunting Legendary Rifles ASSOULINE

Designer James Farmer and his team took on the challenge of taking a nearly 100-year-old home and updating it for a young family. The house is a revival of Southern Federal style and is nestled on a sprawling family peach farm. The family room sofas are covered in stunning velvet, and the variety of patterns used throughout the room complement each other.

PLACE TO CALL HOME
FARMER
Private Edens
BEAUTIFUL COUNTRY GARDENS

Italian majolica lamps add a classic flair that still reflects the youth and fun of the home's family. Opposite: The foyer frames a lovely view into the dining room. The natural sunlight streams in and highlights the well-curated pieces.

The sunroom features quintessential Southern elements such as rattan, wicker, and blue on the ceiling. Farmer selected indoor/outdoor fabrics, a tone-on-tone Oushak rug, and plenty of plants and flowers to add texture and layering.

The kitchen features a butcher block-topped island and rattan barstools. A former passage and pantry was transformed into a wet bar.

The other end of the sunroom was given a table and chairs to serve as overflow from the dining room.

Sunny Disposition

Bigger is not always better, particularly in interior design. Although spacious rooms and soaring ceilings often rank high on a homebuyer's most wanted list, they can present challenges when it comes to giving interiors a warm, cozy vibe. "When my clients purchased their 10-year-old home in 2020, their goal was to make it feel warm and welcoming despite its generous footprint," says interior designer Sandra Lucas of Lucas/Eilers Design Associates. "We had worked with them on their previous homes, and it was important for us to achieve a fresh look that matched their friendly spirit and joyful outlook."

According to Lucas, the home's "great bones" are what attracted her clients to the brick manse in Houston's tiny Memorial neighborhood. Rich architectural details, including molding, shiplap, and coffered ceilings, convey character and add texture along with the antique Coffeyville brick and reclaimed wood. But its heavy lighting, stained paneling, and layers of brown and beige made the interior look too dark and dated. Lucas softened spaces by whitewashing some of the wood and stone elements and introducing a punchy palette ranging from cool blues and greens to warm corals and yellows. Even the light fixtures were revived—not replaced—and hand-painted in a champagne finish. "Choosing hues that play well together is the key to successfully designing a home filled with color," Lucas says.

For Lucas, achieving a harmonious flow of color was key. She used colored pencils to sketch the floor plan and determine how hues would transition from room to room. By balancing vibrant colors with neutral tones, she created visual rest and a sense of balance—an essential element in design. "Balance is what makes us feel good about our built environments," Lucas says.

Pattern balance was also a priority. In the breakfast room, she paired a solid, textured fabric for the chairs with the bold printed grasscloth wallcovering. In the dining room, she used solid wool fabric for the chair fronts to highlight the Fortuny-patterned backs. Throughout the home, Lucas blended classic and contemporary pieces, incorporating antiques from the homeowners' collection, including consoles, commodes, and tables. A striking 18th-century Welsh dresser, showcasing marbleized Christopher Spitzmiller dinnerware, anchors the dining room. The simple form and playful pattern of the display add youthfulness, contrasting with the formality of the dresser.

"The beauty of this home is in the mix," Lucas says. "You can feel the history that overflows from the reclaimed finishes and antique furnishings—every nick and imperfection tell a story. But the modern art and accessories also tell a story, and it recounts the authentic style and youthful spirit of the family who call it home." By blending past and present, Lucas achieved a design that's both timeless and personal.

De Gournay panels welcome guests and impart whimsy in the otherwise formal foyer. Comfy chairs upholstered in a floral damask print surround a game table. The fabric's soft blue-greens, creams, and golds lighten up the space with notes of apricot tying it all together.

For the library, Lucas reversed the living room palette, and gallery walls feature antique maps from the homeowners' travels. Moody blue grasscloth wraps the walls of the dining room and highlights the limestone fireplace. The arched mirror and Iatesta Studio branch light fixture soften the straight lines of the furniture.

The breakfast room's white-on-taupe floral wallcovering is a perfect transition between the rich tones of the brick-clad kitchen and the apricot paneled living room. A reclaimed brick grotto and custom range hood create a focal point in the kitchen. Kate Spade's Bella Books wallcovering climbs the walls of the laundry room.

AUDREY HEPBURN
BREAKFAST AT TIFFANY'S

The daughter's bathroom features a punchy abstract wallcovering by Pierre Frey. A cheerful palette of yellow, coral, and teal is featured in the floral headboard and the Missoni rug.

A delicate chinoiserie wallcovering tempers the hardy reclaimed brick floors in the lady's bath and dressing room. The 1950s-style slipper chair was custom designed with a higher seat so that it sits at just the right height for the vanity. The GP & J Baker fabric that covers the headboard is between a toile and a botanical print. A rich green welt winds the edge of the headboard to accentuate its unique scalloped silhouette. Subtle hues of khaki, sand, and seafoam are also derived from its earthy palette and are repeated on the drapes, settee, and painted bedside chests.

CURATED

Modern History

Following in the footsteps of his family, a homeowner of a Georgian estate in Chevy Chase, Maryland, approached designer Barry Dixon and architect Geri Yantis to give his sprawling abode the aesthetic and practicalities he dreamed of. The owner, a former city dweller with a love for hunting and outdoor living, wanted his home to reflect his lifestyle while incorporating modern sensibilities. Dixon carefully mixed progressive, masculine designs with inherited, traditional furnishings, ensuring the space was both functional and welcoming for the owner's two Labrador retrievers.

The foyer, bathed in natural light, opens to the study, dining room, and living room. A round table, commissioned from London, with three solid bronze legs and a decoupaged guinea fowl feather design, is a focal point. An antique lantern hangs from the grasscloth-covered ceiling, and a floor-to-ceiling mirror, placed on the floor, enhances the space, reflecting light and creating a sense of openness. Multiple seating areas ensure easy flow for larger gatherings.

In the living room, a custom rug complements the dark floors and outdoor views. Velvet-covered swivel chairs provide comfort for TV viewing, while a game table and brass sofa table add to the rich, warm atmosphere. The ceiling coffers are trimmed with bronze nailheads, creating a quiet and inviting space. Dixon also included Greek and Irish elements, honoring the owner's heritage, such as a hand-carved 18th-century piece of Zeus in the study and a stone pillar with a gilded eagle.

Continuing the theme of bringing the outdoors in, the dining room was given a wallcovering that features trees and foliage, alongside a custom light fixture resembling natural leaves. Another floor-to-ceiling mirror reflects the wallcovering, while leather dining chairs enhance the masculine vibe. "I wanted this room to feel like you were dining within the natural landscape," Dixon says. The kitchen mixes light and dark finishes and includes three distinct seating areas, with a tall, round table by the island perfect for entertaining.

The owner's suite blends modern and antique elements, with family heirloom dressers and an iron bed surrounded by a seating area on a natural wool carpet. French doors lead to the upper terrace, and the walls feature the owner's collection of hunting prints on herringbone-patterned panels. "The goal was to curate the heavier French antiques with more modern, clean pieces," he says. "That careful mix is really what brought this home to life and gave it the exact feel the owner wanted."

Furniture placement within the spacious foyer was given careful consideration, as designer Barry Dixon wanted it to be a welcoming, hospitable space for guests.

The warm study includes a leather Chesterfield sofa, the owner's cherished collection of books, and accents that reflect his Greek and Irish heritage. The foyer's round table was commissioned from London and features bronze legs and a top decoupaged with guinea fowl feathers. Dixon added a custom, deep green banquette with fringe trim that can comfortably seat four people.

The large rug in the living room is a custom design of Dixon's. It was specially dyed to match the surrounding trees and the dark floors within the space. The draperies are hand block printed on recycled cotton and linen.

The kitchen is made up of three separate spaces in one: a breakfast room, main kitchen and bar area, and a seating area with four chairs and a daybed. The mix of light and dark finishes keep the atmosphere masculine and clean, while details like high-back swivel chairs and a New Zealand shag rug allow for plenty of comfort.

The primary suite is a blend of heavier antique pieces and modern, elegant accents. The minimal iron bed allows the antique bedside dressers to feel natural, while the textured walls create softness and warmth.

COLOR IN YOUR GARDEN
FRAGILE DIPLOMACY
WILLIAM SEALE
North American Indian
ANNE GEDDES
Until Now
life in a tuscan town

Fresh Start

Our clients wanted a house convenient to friends and with enough room for entertaining inside and out, as well as bedrooms for their growing family of grandchildren," says designer Carter Kay. Empty nesters eager for change, the couple found a 1940s Craftsman bungalow that offered the perfect setting for their next phase of life. Nestled in the Garden Hills neighborhood, the house boasted old heart pine floors, plaster walls, and the smaller, defined rooms of a previous era. Kay, who'd worked with the couple on their previous house, took on the challenge to reimagine uses for cherished pieces and give their new home a bright, fresh look.

Avid collectors, the couple especially love the work of Ed Moulthrop, world-renowned woodturner. In the living room, a piece by Moulthrop takes pride of place on a library table, surrounded by books that reflect the owners' passion for art and history. "Because they value antiques and love history, they like combining family heirlooms with current furniture and artifacts," says Kay. A mixture of pretty antiques and contemporary notes, like the Federal-style mirror flanked by modern sconces, merge wide-ranging sensibilities in a timeless fashion. "The crystal chandelier and table were our clients' first dining set, and we decided to put a fresh spin on them here," says Kay.

In the dining room, the couple's passions are on full display, with antique mirrors and French chairs mingled with a glass-and-acrylic table. The wall covering is notable for its vaguely ikat design and energizing effect. "Knowing we would need a concentrated jolt of color and pattern, we commissioned the paper from a company in Arkansas," says Kay.

African elements add depth to the design. In the side entry, an African bench is covered in a fabric resembling a zebra stripe. "With the Persian rug, the disparate elements have fun playing with each other," says Kay. In the family room, among the playful notes of vivid orange swivel chairs and ratchet arm benches, an African child's chair lends a sculptural note to the arrangement. On display around the house are handmade baskets and textiles that speak to a well-traveled aesthetic, like the kitchen table runner, a geometric patterned cloth suggestive of a far-flung market find.

Elsewhere, Kay designed shallow shelving on the paneled landing to accommodate a collection of beer steins. In the kitchen, cabinetry features a niche to display Tadelakt pottery from Morocco. An enormous key suspended from the ceiling was a serendipitous find. "We knew the kitchen was missing something, even after all the planning and arranging of accessories," says Kay. "My assistant, Nancy, found this key at a local flea market on installation day, and we realized it was the linchpin for the whole house."

With the wide-ranging collections, dynamic mix of old and new, and timeless architectural detail, the house looks like it naturally evolved over time. But for the clients, seeing their beloved treasures in a fresh setting is a brand-new experience.

North American Indian
color in VENICE

A mix of textures enlivens the cool tones of the living room, with leather, velvet, and linen offering tactile interest. An acrylic coffee table adds a modern note.

The dining room's impactful wallpaper was designed by Arkansas artisans to offer contrast to the living room's cool mood. A glass-and-acrylic table surrounded by traditional chairs takes the formality down a notch, along with contemporary touches like the wall sconces.

A curved cased opening frames the breakfast room and bar. Industrial metal notes in the shelving and light fixture lend an airiness to the kitchen. Kay used concrete for the kitchen counters, with leathered marble on the island.

ANSEL ADAMS
NATIONAL GEOGRAPHIC Atlas of the World

In the family room, a roughly striped rug is forgiving of spills. Orange swivel chairs add a pop of color and can turn toward the kitchen. Rather than using window seats, Kay placed a pair of ratchet arm benches beneath the windows. A leather wing chair adds a masculine touch.

In the bedroom, an 18th-century English chest, mid-century bedside tables and lamps, antique Spanish library table, and Regency drinks table all live together harmoniously.

Couture Chic

In decorating, good things often come to those who wait, especially when they wait for those defining qualities that make for a unique home. "After all, Rome wasn't built in a day," says Charlotte interior designer Kathy Smith. "We took the long view in the design and were in no hurry to have it 'finished' in that sense." Smith and one of her favorite clients enjoyed the hunt and pleasure in locating one-of-a-kind finds and arresting accents.

Some of those finds grace the living room, which illustrates how an understated palette can be beautifully engaging with its mix of appointments—dramatic antique coach torches accompany crystal sconces; a multifaceted large chandelier provides definition in a sitting area; a framed kimono serves as art over a custom sofa; while an impeccably patinaed bench holds court nearby.

In the family room, a color shift comes into play. "Here we decided to be a little brave," says Smith. "We ventured out with a gold for the window treatments and a shade of chartreuse for the velvet upholstery." The designer didn't stop there, injecting a lively purple-hued silk damask for accent pillows. "While the room is still full of antiques, the chosen colors add a note of informality—a don't-take-yourself-too-seriously attitude," she says. Brushstrokes of green flow throughout the home, providing a link between the spaces.

The kitchen was completely reimagined during the redesign. Rather than a traditional marble-topped island, Smith chose a vintage French drapery table to define the space. An antique chandelier replaces the expected pendant, and open shelving brings airiness to the room while displaying art and decorative pieces. The adjoining breakfast area features a custom gold-striped banquette, slipcovered chairs, and another antique chandelier.

While every room reveals layers of beauty, Smith imbued the elegant dining room with a special allure. In the dining room, the designer chose a luxurious muted silk paper for the walls and commissioned the well-known Charlotte artist Terry Reitzel to paint a botanical-themed mural in warm shades of green mixed with murky neutrals. To ensure this paper remained the star in the room, Smith painted all the existing built-ins and trim an earthy hue with yellow undertones reminiscent of the varied colors in aged bamboo, which draws the eye toward the mural.

The designer's deft hand in pairing somewhat unexpected colors is on full display in the primary bedroom as well. Eschewing the classic mix of soothing neutrals, Smith joined a chalky gray tone for the walls with shades of tangerine and bright ocher and a combination of wood finishes. This mix envelops the room creating a cocooning effect, which is remarkably serene in its presentation. Noteworthy antique finds join in, such as an Italian chair, a Fortuny standing lamp, and an octagon-shaped floor mirror with intricate detailing.

"This home reflects the best of the best—we never compromised," says Smith. The homeowner adds, "It's been a wonderful journey with Kathy to see my home evolve into a place to relax as well as entertain, and seeing everything come together has been magical."

Luxurious élan is at play in the living room with glorious antiques, tactile fabrics, and well-edited objets d'art that shine against creamy walls in Benjamin Moore's Linen White and a neutral-hued rug.

The dining room's elegance shines through with hand-painted wallcovering and dining chairs with graceful lines in a silk Nancy Corzine textile. Dripping in rich color, the family room presents a layered mélange of textures with patinaed finishes, sumptuous fabrics, and a glimmering chandelier.

LOUIS VUITTON
May I Come In?
CAROLYNE ROEHM DESI
The Private World of Yves Saint Laurent & Pierre Bergé

A gold striped custom banquette, tailored slipcovered chairs, and a streamlined Baker table are featured in the breakfast space. The kitchen's overhaul brought in pretty cabinets painted in Sherwin-Williams Porpoise along with the gleaming range and vent hood.

Creating Home
KEITH SUMMEROUR

Trimmed glass-front cabinets and paintings by Felice Sharp and Louis Shields hang in the bar. The library is saturated in color for a calming retreat .

A decidedly chic main bathroom features marble floors, an antique chair, and a crystal chandelier. Enviable décor in the main bedroom includes a velvet bed covering, a sinuous Baker chaise, and an antique upholstered bench.

RETREATS

Seaside Sophistication

For years, longtime clients of interior designer Carolyn Kendall, owner of Alcott Interiors, coveted a house in Boca Grande, Florida, where they owned a condo. The property, with its stunning beach, panoramic water views, and ample acreage, was irresistible. When the house finally came up for sale, the clients seized the opportunity, though the one-story home needed a complete makeover. "We gutted the entire house; only the facade stayed the same," says Kendall. The homeowners enlisted Nashville architect Ron Farris to collaborate with Kendall on the design.

While the house needed major changes, it did offer a few gems. One was a paneled antique living room imported from Europe by the former owners. Though the ceiling was too dark for the beach house vibe the clients envisioned, Kendall lightened it using a limewash technique. To preserve the integrity of the stained wood, she padded the walls lightly before reupholstering them. A built-in glass-front cabinet that had showcased the previous owners' shell collection also came with the house. Kendall updated it by wallpapering the back of the shelves to match the surrounding walls, creating a seamless look.

The clients had personal touches they wanted to add, such as two hand-painted tile fireplaces. In the living room, the tiles depicted coastal elements like fish, shells, and lighthouses, while the upstairs bedroom featured tiles with portraits of family members and pets. A custom coffee table, filled with shells collected by the homeowners, added another personal element to the design.

Antiques sourced both locally and abroad gave the house a refined yet not overly formal elegance. Key pieces included shell mirrors, a patinaed English console, and a lamp made from a Parisian antique fragment. Kendall also commissioned custom pieces, such as bedside chests from London-based Justin Van Breda and wall sconces from Urban Electric. The low ceiling heights in most rooms were a challenge, but Kendall creatively addressed this by hanging window treatments high and incorporating eye-catching light fixtures like a blue Murano chandelier to draw the eye upward.

A blue-and-white color palette was central to the design, reflecting the clients' desire for a fresh yet timeless feel. "It is blue-and-white to the nines," says Kendall, noting that the varying shades of blue and diverse patterns throughout the home keep the space dynamic. This color scheme was carried through with wallpaper, striped and floral fabrics for upholstered headboards and dining chairs, and tiles in the bathroom. The kitchen featured a painted island and upholstered bar chairs, showcasing a brighter blue hue. In the family room, bold blue lacquered wallpaper covered custom built-ins and walls, while in the sunroom, blue is more of a supporting player, letting the ocean views take a starring role. After all, the location was always the main attraction.

Throughout the house, the careful blend of new and old elements—paired with the stunning location—created a coastal retreat that was both stylish and deeply personal.

THE BUCKET LIST
THE SEASIDE HOUSE

The living room is wrapped in a pretty palm print fabric—Pasha from Lisa Fine Textiles—and has a lighthearted attitude that plays well against the antique beams, ceiling, and doors imported from Europe.

The dining room appointments include chairs in a handsome blue Pierre Frey fabric, a Murano glass chandelier, and shell-encrusted mirror. The family room's crisp allure comes from deep blue lacquer wallpaper from Phillip Jeffries and Alan Campbell floral window panels. Touches of aqua in pillows and cornice boards link the room to nearby spaces.

A cozy sunroom off the living room has ocean views with pale aqua shades and handwoven rope furnishings from John Himmel. The back porch is another spot to take in the views with comfortable pieces from Century Furniture. The table is set for alfresco dining with Drucker Paris rattan bistro chairs.

The lively kitchen renovation has a casual coastal vibe with Brunschwig & Fils zigzag print barstools and perky aqua blue kitchenware, which pop against the white backdrop.

ABERLOUR

A guest room has an enviable setting with outdoor access. The room's sitting area is decorated with drapery panels and a pillow from Carleton V, Ltd.

The spacious main suite with ocean views includes an engaging mix of textures through fabrics and accent pieces, like a marquetry side table and a hand-painted fireplace tile surround.

Room to Grow

There is no such thing as an empty nest for Patty Thomas and Henry Waszkowski. The Atlanta-based couple met and married later in life, each with children and grandchildren of their own spread across the South. With their newly blended family in the double digits, the couple quickly realized that the best way to foster a tight family unit would be to have a place spacious enough for multiple generations to gather comfortably. "There's no greater joy than having everyone under one roof for long weekends and holidays, but we didn't have a place large enough to accommodate everyone," Thomas says.

Much like they embraced a new chapter in life, Thomas and Waszkowski embraced a new project—the design and construction of a 5,000-square-foot home in the quaint community of Cashiers. Situated on a coveted level lot overlooking the Blue Ridge Mountains, the house has the enchanting appeal of a centuries-old structure nestled deep into the Black Forest or French Alps.

For the exterior, Charlotte-based architect T. Mark Paullin sourced European-inspired materials, such as western red cedar siding and roof shakes, as well as rugged orchard stone quarried from West Virginia and Tennessee. He also incorporated authentic architectural elements like the asymmetrical window arrangement and the gently arched portico that welcomes guests as they approach the custom Dutch door.

To continue the European ambiance indoors, Thomas and Waszkowski enlisted interior designer Francie Hargrove. Known for her French Country aesthetic, Hargrove chose a soft white hue for the Venetian plaster walls as a clean counterpoint to the paneled ceiling comprised of antique pine. Blackened bronze, steel-framed windows punctuate the neutral backdrop and draw the eye outside to pristine views. Typical of any European mountain home, a grand limestone fireplace stands proudly in the living room.

While some of the antiques were purchased during travels to France, many of them were sourced directly from the homeowner's existing inventory. A thoughtful collection of paintings and prints in chippy gilded frames speaks to the homeowners' affinity for art, and their love of color is evidenced in the saturated shades of persimmon, amber, ochre, and sage throughout the house. "People talk a lot about bringing the outdoors in, and that's exactly what we did with these hues," Hargrove says. "The earth tones and wood tones that we used were inspired by the landscape, and so were the natural textures we layered throughout the interior. Sisal rugs, linen curtains, and upholstered pieces in wool, leather, and mohair evoke a sense of rusticity, but they are balanced with finery to make the overall appeal a bit more regal."

The living room's massive limestone mantel was custom-designed to support the 18th-century painted trumeau mirror that hangs above it. The custom wrought-iron railing in the stairwell was replicated from a photograph that the owners took at a hotel during a visit to Bonnieux, France.

To keep the all-white kitchen from looking stark, the inset cabinets and gracious island are hand-glazed in a coffee color and topped with honed quartzite countertops that evoke a timeworn patina. In the dining room, a palette of rich browns, muted greens, and burnished golds capitalize on the colors of the woodland views. Hargrove dressed the windows in a traditional botanical-damask print that echoes the leafy treetops and downplays the more modern steel-framed windows.

Death & Co

Chocolate-brown walls, a painted leather screen, and an antler-base ottoman impart a masculine tone in the study, while a cheetah-print rug lends a youthful vibe. A spacious, all-weather porch features retractable screens that open to impart an alfresco ambiance when it's warm.

A sunburst-shaped antique Italian architectural fragment hangs in the center of an arched niche in the master suite. At the base of the niche is a built-in chest that holds the television on a stand that rises and recesses with a remote control when not in use. "The shiplap walls help tone down the formality and femininity of the master suite," Hargrove says. A canopy made from custom-colored Peter Fasano fabric adds a layer of luxury to the private retreat.

Southern Coastal Living
GARDENS
STYLE AND SUBSTANCE
ALL SEASONS

The Magic of the Marsh

It only took one 20-minute visit to this South Carolina property for Nicole Lynch and her husband, William, to sign a contract with the realtor. "It's a magical place," Lynch says, noting their family's love of the outdoors and fishing. The couple were taken with this house specifically due to its location at the tip of a point in Sea Pines Resort, offering a sweeping view of the marsh. The property, which they named Lawton Landing, offered sweeping views of the marsh and the daily activity on Lawton Creek. Despite the house being renovated by previous owners, the Lynches wanted a refresh that aligned with their family's style and the home's surroundings. To achieve this, they enlisted Atlanta-based designer Amy Morris.

For this project, Morris paired Nicole's love of antiques and expertly curated fabrics with subtle nods to the nautical setting through textures and accessories. "For me, it's always about creating a look that fits my client," Morris says. The vision starts at the front door where a painted cabinet and rope-framed mirror, both antiques, set the tone for what's to come. "We wanted to find a standout piece and also introduce the home's textures the fibers, the sheers on the windows, and the coral—in the entry as a clue to what you can expect to see throughout," Morris says. Blue hues also hint at the palette that flows from space to space

Morris, known for her ability to tailor designs to her clients, integrated Nicole's love for antiques and carefully curated fabrics while adding subtle nautical influences through textures and accessories. A standout piece in the entry—a painted antique cabinet and rope-framed mirror—sets the tone for the home, introducing fibers, sheers, and coral accents, as well as the home's blue color palette.

Morris, known for her ability to tailor designs to her clients, incorporated local art into a gallery wall, sourcing pieces over the course of a year-long makeover. Throughout the home, accents like tortoise shells and oyster baskets evoke the area's natural beauty. Morris also considered the Lynches' three children, selecting durable furniture and whimsical pieces, such as pairing an antique chair with a modern acrylic desk in the youngest daughter's room.

Attention to detail was paramount, from fabric selection to customizations like button closures on pillows and fanciful tie closures on bedding and drapery. The Lynches also wanted the home to be a place for hosting, and the design reflects a vacation vibe. A bold circus-striped wallpaper in the dining room, initially a risk, became a favorite, making the space feel like a festive getaway, even though it's a formal dining room.

Outside, the family enjoys their dock, which stretches into the marsh, for cocktail hour and dinner, enhancing the home's retreat-like atmosphere. Morris's thoughtful design transformed the property into a cozy, elegant space that feels like a vacation home, blending coastal charm with personal style and family-friendly practicality.

The artwork in the living room, Returning 52 by Tom Swanson, is reflective of the scenes often viewed from the marsh dock. Filled with light and stunning views, Morris opted to paint the formerly dark walls of the living room in classic White Dove by Benjamin Moore but left the stained beams intact for contrast. The spacious room is divided into two seating areas that are united by a light palette and natural fiber rug.

In the entry, an understated coastal look is introduced through numerous textures and marine-inspired accents. Commissioned photographs of the property by Rob Brinson now serve as art in the living and dining rooms. Located off the entry hall with access to the dining room, the bar is a hub for entertaining. To soften the design, fabric—rather than tile—covers the base of the cabinetry and backsplash. Located just off the entry, the media room is draped in blackout panels that close to create a cozy viewing space.

In the dining room, a striped wallpaper from Cole & Son sets a playful tone that also hints at the home's coastal setting. Upholstered host chairs and a laminated fabric on the side chairs speak to the home's practicality and durability, while an antique Swedish Gustavian-style table grounds the space. A painted armoire holds pieces from Nicole's creamware collection.

In the owners' bedroom, an iron bed by Mr. and Mrs. Howard for Sherrill Furniture mixes with an antique bench, table, and serpentine commodes that act as bedside tables. "Nicole has amazing taste in antiques, and we would often send pictures back and forth when shopping," Morris says of her client. Near the front entry, a courtyard with palm trees is emblematic of the home's Lowcountry style.

Acknowledgments

CLASSIC

12 Classic Collaboration: Interior design, Barbara Westbrook, Barbara Westbrook Interiors. Architecture, Keith Summerour. Photography, Erica George Dines.

24 Island Style: Interior design, Will Huff, Huff-Dewberry. Architecture, Spitzmiller & Norris. Photography, Jessie Preza, Photo & Style.

40 To the Manor Born: Architecture, Stan Dixon, D. Stanley Dixon. Interior design, Jackye Lanham, Jacquelynne P. Lanham Designs. Photography, Eric Piasecki. *Home: The Residential Architecture of D. Stanley Dixon*, by D. Stanley Dixon. Rizzoli ©2024

EUROPEAN

54 Passport to Italy: Interior design, John Oetgen, Oetgen Design. Photography, Emily Followill.

68 French Influence: Interior design, Cathy Kincaid, Cathy Kincaid Interiors. Photography, Michael Hunter.

78 All in the Mix: Interior design, Ann Wolf, Wolf Holden Design Studio. Photography, Chris Luker.

MODERN

92 Color Craving: Interior design, Janie Molster, Janie Molster Designs. Photography, Mali Azima. *House Dressing: Interiors for Colorful Living* by Janie Molster, Monacelli Press ©2021

108 All About the Views: Interior design, Mary Douglas Drysdale, Mary Douglas Drysdale Interior Design. Photography, John Cole.

118 Big Easy Breezy: Interior design, Katie Scott, Katie Scott Design. Photography, Tria Giovan.

COLORFUL

132 Classic Meets Colorful: Interior design, Edith-Anne Duncan, Edith-Anne Duncan Design. Photography, Dustin Peck. *Southern Sensibility* by Edith-Anne Duncan, Gibbs Smith ©2025

146 Passion for Color: Interior design, Kelley Proxmire, Kelley Proxmire, Inc. Photography, Kip Dawkins.

158 Carolina Calling: Interior design, James Farmer, James Farmer Interior Design. Photography, Jeff Herr. *Arriving Home* by James Farmer, Gibbs Smith ©2020

170 Sunny Disposition: Interior design, Sandy Lucas, Lucas-Eilers Interior Design. Photography, Stephen Karlisch. *Expressive Interiors: Designing an Inviting Home* by Sandra Lucas and Sarah Eilers, Rizzoli ©2020

CURATED

184 Modern History: Interior design, Barry Dixon, Barry Dixon Interiors. Photography, Gordon Beall.

196 Fresh Start: Interior design, Carter Kay, Carter Kay Interiors. Photography, Emily Followill.

208 Couture Chic: Interior design, Kathy Smith, Kathy Smith Interiors. Photography: Brie Williams.

RETREATS

222 Seaside Sophistication: Interior design, Carolyn Kendall, Alcott Interiors. Photography, Emily Followill.

236 Room to Grow: Interior design, Francie Hargrove, Francie Hargrove Interior Design. Photography, Emily Followill.

246 The Magic of the Marsh: Interior design, Amy Morris, Amy Morris Interiors. Photography, Erica George Dines.

End sheets & chapter openers by Paul Montgomery Mural Source.